SAME

LIFE

SAME

MAUREEN N. McLANE

FARRAR, STRAUS AND GIROUX NEW YORK

FARRAR, STRAUS AND GIROUX
18 West 18th Street, New York 10011

Distributed in Canada by Douglas & McIntyre Ltd.
Printed in the United States of America
First edition, 2008

Library of Congress Cataloging-in-Publication Data
McLane, Maureen N.
    Same life / Maureen N. McLane.— 1st ed.
        p. cm.
    ISBN-13: 978-0-374-16533-8 (hardcover : alk. paper)
    ISBN-10: 0-374-16533-5 (hardcover : alk. paper)
    I. Title.

PS3613.M2728 2008
811'.6—dc22
                                        2007047957

Designed by Quemadura

www.fsgbooks.com

1 3 5 7 9 10 8 6 4 2

Life is, generally speaking, a blessing independent of a future state.

——T. R. MALTHUS, *An Essay on the Principle of Population*

Spare us from loveliness. ——H.D., "Orchard"

CONTENTS

I

were fragments enough . . . 3

unmeasured the white . . . 5

Catechism 6

never so free . . . 8

after guston 9

Catches for Robert Duncan 10

The Daily Failures . . . 11

after sappho:
I some say . . . 12
II I would rather see . . . 13
III neither the women of the city rising . . . 14
IV it's true the charm may lie . . . 15
V and you / whom I will likely never see . . . 16

in my head a little groove . . . 18

From Mʒ N: the serial 19

II

regional 31

the special stasis of august . . . 32

Poem 33

Citizens 35

Letter from Paris 38

Report 42

This is the worst country . . . 44

pitigliano 45

the sun slips below . . . 46

saratoga 47

the sex of the stars . . . 48

songs of a season 49

stars arranging . . . 55

III

after guston II 59

Tenancy 60

MAYAKOVSKY at High Table 62

Terrible things are happening / in Russian novels! . . . 64

My dearest Lavinia . . . 66

to a poet renowned for a certain sensualism 67

Spatchcocked 69

Excursion Susan Sontag 71

IV

Populating Heaven 79

There is a place . . . 81

At the end, a door 82

lying face / down . . . 89

syntax 90

song 91

early music at the coffee shop 92

V

I wanted to crawl inside a middle voice . . . 95

mist lowering the scrim . . . 96

symphony / in the air . . . 97

notational / sufficiency . . . 98

cumuli gathering low . . . 99

was he right the poet . . . 100

same view . . . 101

Core Samples
When I met you I was eighteen . . . 102
Those were the years . . . 103
It was under the spell of Yeats . . . 103
You I never fell in love with . . . 104
I never made you breakfast . . . 105
Sad in bed you read Horace . . . 106

do I still turn to them . . . 107

in the end a windblown woman am I . . . 108

Envoi 109

NOTES 111

ACKNOWLEDGMENTS 113

were fragments enough . . .

were fragments enough
for a life

for a fiction
of continuity

in our every cell
a tiny alphabet restricts itself

to the possible
mutations,

evolution
proceeding along lines

imperceptible
as the day

I was thrown
from the imaginary car

& broke the barrier
of this carrying life

it is true I take pleasure
annihilating all the world

to a penned thought caught
in a fan's whirring blade

unmeasured the white . . .

unmeasured the white
you write on

unbothered your breath
when you sleep

paradise caught in the ear
its cartilaginous shell

become a night bell

Catechism

Did your mother like you
    She was afraid of me

And the kindergarten
    Glowed like the yellow sno-cone

And the dingding man
    Was gentle kind & true

How old are you
    This is my last incarnation

Where did you first see the morning glory
    Sometime before the millennium but long after I had
        grown up

What foods
    Chicken pizza powdered milk

What foods
    Vegetable biryani flautas falafel asparagus turbot

And then
> I fell in love three times each time was violent and small
> things smashed and bloomed

What world
> The place I live is only sometimes shareable thus weeping

And after
> That day I realized calm that something tremendous had
> happened to me but I had not noticed

Diagramming sentences
> For a long time I used to go to bed early

Finally a beginning
> There is one day it will all end for me

never so free . . .

never so free as after the death

of heaven, the sun's shaft loosed

from the sky, its wheel unhitching

the blue as it darkens, burns

black and I, and I, and I

almost fall in the vale, the first cry

tearing the mouth

after guston

a little patch of green
    is all I've seen

the gray field overlaid
    with strokes unmade

by a practiced hand

    souls massed by the wall
    the unclaimed dead their legs
        boneless, nailed

        to the ladder the painter
        climbs every night

        in his spider-webbed sleep

Catches for Robert Duncan

              The century has barely rung
its cold clear notes of morning, has scarcely flashed
its signs across the neoned globe and desert space
when every tower swaying in the air broadcasts
a beautiful menace. The northern birds have heard
the ice crack and seep in the Arctic and elsewhere
a hand is upraised even now to strike. The sharp
slap the gunner's blast the houses smashed
by tanks ingenious engineers designed, the smelters
and welders long had their work cut out. Lilies
slowly unfurl their ahistorical petals while olives
and grapes look for harvest and women cry
calling their children home. Old gods speak
in script and what they say brushes the desert red.

The Daily Failures . . .

The daily failures are piling in heaps
        at the ends of all driveways
                and no one is sure there's recycling.

Who's to say
        with a perfect love perfected
                we would not live forever?

In some heaven the saints are conversing
        so fluently the very birds understand
                their speech is song.

after sappho I

some say a host of horsemen, a horizon of ships
under sail is most beautiful but I say it is whatever
you love I say it is
you

after sappho II

I would rather see your face
than all . . .

after sappho III

neither the women of the city rising
over the lake nor those of the
medieval towns
shining on the riverred island nor
the beauties floating down these gridded
taxi'd streets nor any
man ever
is pleasing to my
eyes but
you

after sappho IV

it's true the charm may lie
        somewhat
  in the subject such as gardens
                wedding songs love affairs
against these few will speak and all
              at one time
     may have hoped—
but there is your bending
      neck and the small hollow at the base
        of your long back
      and no charm
       other

song likes its own delights and even sadness
    in some modes
         charms
              those whose hearts have moved
         so

      what to do with the soul
              its many
                  motions

after sappho V

and you
whom I will likely never see again
I hope it has all gone well
      that the lover has finally left his wife
      that roses now climb the trellis you'd staked
      and you've left the less-than-stellar job—
      —perhaps everything is changed

you deserved every gift
      you never got and all the ones
        you did. you led so many
        onward and if when they arrived
          they found themselves
            alone, aflame—

        you above all know I was left
        so, my insides ash—

        why blame the fire
        for its damage?
        for so long it gave a lovely light—

and when I last saw you
       and you so lightly said
             o wait there love   o wait a moment love
          how could that bird
             in my throat
                 tho I had snuffed that all out
                             not revive

in my head . . .

in my head a little groove
you made one night
a diamond cut the vinyl raw
and I saw

From Mz N: the serial

Like all children Mz N lived
in archaic
mythic zones
and all the neighbors and kin played their parts to a T
although they never were able to tell her
the whole story.

§

The child Mz N sat on her bed
and wondered: that tree
outside her window
shifted
when her eye
shifted. What to make
of that?

§

Mz N and her siblings
had a dog for some time.
They went on vacation &

when they came back
no dog.
They asked the parents:
the dog?
who replied:
what dog?
And some people wonder
why others distrust the obvious.

§

One year Mz N began her great project
of investigative
touch. Like everything
it came about
through reading
and happenstance. Mz N had a friend
who said I do it and then
I worry
what if my roommate
hears?
What if?
Mz N wondered
went home
and discovered a new octave.

§

Mz N sometimes thinks
what N stands for: Nothing.
One day she said
nīhilism
in school & the teacher
paused, chalk between her fingers
like her longed-for cigarette.
What's nīhilism
another student said I thought
it was *neehilism*.
This was another example
of Mz N bringing up topics
that went Nowhere.

§

the blackest black
is not so black
it cannot take
a blacker black

so Mz N thinks
the void would speak
if void could speak
or of color think

§

21

Mz N is writing what she hopes will be
a masterpiece: *Mispronunciation:*
the definitive
autobiography. She only includes
the bloopers she remembers.
She is very strict like that.
What's vá-gi-na
—hard *g*—
she called to her parents
age five
when they'd plopped her on the sofa
with a picture book
to help her learn
where babies. Some years later she told a story
at dinner
about being very angry
with a persecuting
teacher. I spoke
she sd
with great ve-hé-mence.
Her father laughed
a somewhat unkind laugh
and asked her to repeat it.
She did & once again
he laughed.
Mz N vehemently

objects to the making fun of children
who struggle every day
to get their words
and bodies aligned

§

one day after sex
in a century of bad sex
the other one asked Mz N
did I leave you
on the edge
never having had an orgasm
as far as she knew
she sd
quite definitively
no
how would she know
such an edge
are you sure
the other persisted
Mz N thought again
she could say
quite definitively
oh yes here I am on the edge
where you left me

the edge
of a certain
abyss
but this
she knew was the answer
to a question
no one was asking

§

Mz N embarks one day upon a sonnet
attracted by the knowledge that it's dead
extinct like dinosaur dodo or bonnet
long replaced by baseball caps on heads

that centuries ago were piled with curls
birds powder wires and such machinery
'twould blow the minds of tattooed boys and girls
who cruise the streets of this new century

Mz N concedes she's antiquarian
old hat old news—"hoarder of ancient dirt"
to quote the mouldy Scot John Pinkerton
but from her dead-end path she won't divert

the airplane made the train a living fossil
relict herself she listens for its whistle

§

Wordsworth never took a plane
but Mz N takes a plane with Wordsworth
on her mind
and other matters: love,
fear, a wish
to die.
Wordsworth had a very sturdy mind
and legs that took him far
into the mountains,
Scottish glens, German
towns and yes across
the Alps. Mz N has never seen
the Alps nor Snowdon
nor a mountain
anywhere beyond the ancient
Adirondacks Wordsworth too she thinks
would like their worndown humps
their pathless woods the rowboats by the shores
of placid lakes ready
for exploring. Young Wordsworth stole
a rowboat
rowed out on a lake one night and found himself
appalled
the mountain strode sublime
after him

and he trembled and his mind
as Burke had said it would
before sublimity
near failed. There are passages
in life
in Wordsworth
he called spots
of time and Mz N has some spots
she sometimes
recollects. But now
she's happy incredulous
in love
and in strange anguish
wants to recollect
nothing. *If it were now*
to die
'twere now to be most happy
she murmurs
with the engine
nearly exploding
with the fragility
and perverse strength of all that lives
and moves and has its being
in the air on the ground in the sea.
Having reached a floating state
of grace, surprised

by joy
she wants to die
life
can only get worse
the mountain
receding below them as they climb

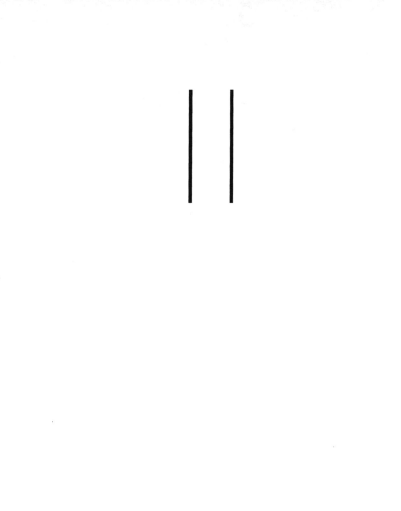

regional

birches by the tracks
beyond them the pines as we rattle by
haven after haven west and new snaking our way
to the first city of the republic
of which the historian of the american south remarked
"if I could live my life in any era
I would choose boston circa 1820"
inspiring diverse thoughts among the students
listening or not as they pleased because pleasure
will make its crooked steel-tied way to the heart
of the assembled population
even in new england

the special stasis of august . . .

the special stasis of august
in the american northeast

this year no drought
to plague the corn

and lawns are often mowed.
in town one hears it said

there's barely been a summer
the rain has washed away the sun

genial complaints at the checkout
a descant above the fat fruit

Poem

As a man may go to Costco,
Buy the jumbo pak of diapers, double liters of
Coke and Diet Coke and a sixpack and stock up on
Doritos and Cheetos and
Evercady batteries, so I perhaps
Formless in the vast republic
Grasp the metaphysical thing, commodity, crucially desired
Hologram of national intent. Caught
In the managed aisle the
Jargon of experts washes o'er the perfectly stacked Special
K, Cheerios, Wheaties, Apple Jacks, and Count Chocula
Low on the shelves that toddlers might harry their
Mothers for sweet breakfast treats. In
Niger the children and livestock go hungry
Once more but a fortified peanut butter paste
Plumpy'nut promises to revive those babies
Quickly who are not yet too far gone.
Research has given us hope that *all*
Shall be well and all manner of thing shall be well
Till the moment it's not. It's not.
Unto the lord Julian of Norwich poured forth her

Voice. Into the desert the Tuareg
Wander, their herds and children starved. Between ocean
Expanses a people of plenty chatter brawl and sometimes
Yawn. Days so short it seems the earth is
Zooming unto its longsought anonymous abyss.

Citizens

I heard you o'er the airwaves
& saw you at last year's
parade—the shorts, sneakers and logo'd T-shirts
the ice cream cones heaped & licked en route
to the best spot for watching
the highschool band and fire dept brigade—
I got dollars in my pocket
       and the mist coming in
          near the ancient boundary between the Algonquin
          and Mohawk and later
the British and French. Route 22
       to me and you
as the topographic grid settles and sets forth imaginary lines
          unto the waters to split the rock called Split Rock
          perhaps since the Treaty of Utrecht.

The vicious little fighting parties
       in brilliant canoes
          the ragtag armies and now
             your SUVs are rollin' on through—

In the landscape of perpetual
        existence and simultaneity
a Persian miniaturist would have the skill
        to formalize & color
we video'd our way from thing
        to thang to thong
and I missed the train
        of historical understanding
        whatever I once thought
that was. Your footnotes
        bore me as do mine,
        and the swooping angels with illumined erasers
        may someday banish commentary
                tho' for now marginalia
                intended or belated
                occasionally has its charms
as when Blake declares I always hate
a smiler and he's a smiling smiler. And still the mist advances
        from the mountain o'er the water to our very own
        shore. This morning

a motorboat cut the lake in two its acrid roar
a backdrop to a phoebe's screech
        —& is it merely class prejudice
                to ban the jetski
instrument of my own brother's pleasure?
        & when a fellow tourist refers to the toilet

at Versailles as a crapper
        must one salute the revolutionary triumph
of the vernacular? There are more bacteria
        in our intestines
than cells in our bodies:
        today's factoid gleaned
from *The New Yorker* and stored
        for a day or two in a neuron or longer
        in a poem.

My brain is stuff'd
wif feeding girls
& boys who glide
from toy to toy
and little stolen brightened joys
whose purity is much alloyed.

Letter from Paris

The French are universal
    particularly in their regard
        for their darker brothers

who under the majesty of the law
    are prohibited equally
        with the white and the rich
    from sleeping under the bridges of Paris.

    The heavy shining stones of the 3rd Republic
and the iron filigree of a thousand balconies
        sing struck by the wind
    & a broom beating a carpet
& the children shout in the playgrounds
    their voices in school
            so ruthlessly suppressed—

The American chain stores have landed
    despite *patrimoine*
    but foie gras persists
        untroubled by the protests
        of Californians

—& surrounded by so much self-evident
            finishing off
        it's hard to resist
    the trimmed leather jacket
    the furcoat that floats by
                as natural as the clouds
    & the roast innards of a
                million beasts gone
        to a long acculturated death.
    If I am out of joint
        it is because I have gone
                completely allegorical
    & my old dreams
        of wholeheartedness
    & a justified life
        have flown out the window
    like yesterday's suicide
                off the Montparnasse Tower.

            It is best to avoid
        grotesque similes but someday
                these likenings
        may become precise
    as the watches the Huguenots perfected
        before they fled
    to the Pays-Bas and South Africa
        & elsewhere

carrying with them a sober intricate knowledge
         of weaving and timepieces
         & the Hebrew Bible.
I am drawing up an indictment
         of the French
         & Reason
         & Human Rights
which begins by unlinking these concepts
     and concludes in weeping.

     Revolution is not only disappointed love Antoine.
There was a time when the earth and every common scene
         featured a green clearing
         where men and women
                  grew strong in their sweet regarding
         each other as fellows and their children
                  newsprung in a
                  new world—

We have written this story again
         and again
and that it was written
         does not make it false
whatever the logic of pastoral
     and its oblique compensations
              for "the real" we never "experience"

—its impossible promise
    of a shepherded life—

the thing was that shining—

let us not put a date
on what now seems forever to be disappearing—

Report

We had heard of the massacres
far away in the interior
of that country an ocean
and a vast inland lake
away. The game was set
for Sunday, a special
program; children were going
to swimming lessons
and the homeless congregated
as usual over the steaming
grates. Those who wished
read the paper, others switched
on their TVs at 11. Dead birds
were the first sign; drowned
cows the second; children banging
their heads against walls
the next and no one
could stop them. In this country
those who could took care
of their pets. The year before
they'd concluded the study

so when the great ash fell
and dusted everyone who'd looked
unknowing to the sky
it fell also on the heaps
of plastic rubbish we had learned
it wasn't safe to burn.

This is the worst country . . .

This is the worst country
        I've ever lived in!
                sd Bill, his beef stroganoff steaming

      and the sangiovese aswirl in the glass

incredulity at ourselves
    our fellow citizens

      the reign of plutocrats   bozos
              and genial thugs

are things worse than ever
      the total world totally gone: imaginable again

      no one minding the store
        driving the car
        stoking the fire
        that's near gone out

      the stolen flame stolen
        for nothing

pitigliano

carved from the hills the city
reaped the rocks' crops—
"of the burial practices of the poor
    we know little"
of the wealthy etruscans, monuments
    and waterworks, the cut
    of a nose, a crown, a fragmentary
    lexicon, a common cup
    a king would casually smash

the sun slips below . . .

the sun slips below
the lowpulled shades

all night the fan's white blades
described a humming circumference

in a dream: the word neon
a political discussion

roasted nuts on a plate
a choice of table linens

some nights even sleep
submits to civilization

saratoga

all day the rain
all night the rain
sheeting the trees

water-battered branches break
      the morning:
      an unmade bed
      a foggy head
yet beyond the fence the blazing horses
      bear the sun

the sex of the stars . . .

the sex of the stars is uncertain
but sure as the sodium
bonds to chlorine
in the precious salt for which lust

the bent rakers harvest
the sea at the Camargue: excrescence
so white so fair come to season
and grace this humble omelette

songs of a season

for here or to go—
a glass mug, a paper cup—
life is fast, art slow

*

only a few years
before all that I am blows
free, subatomic

*

not for me that life
the careless joy of the dog
not for me that leap

*

how to say
beautiful weekend
in chinese?

is "weekend" a concept
in China?

rose petals fell
and the wine uncorked itself
        for our pleasure . . .

                        *

what comfort
do you not give me
little cat?

                        *

wheatfield bleached near blond
light licking the Luberon
and the sea beyond

                        *

the cherry orchard
harvested but for one tree
found that afternoon

                        *

yesterday I saw a fox
    then saw
        it was a deer

all year
    I have been mistaking
        the hunted
            for hunter

                    *

for the lilacs the bees
for the maples the jays
for the locust the chickadee
for the lavender the butterfly
for the bleeding heart the rubythroat
for my lips your tanned throat

                    *

in mandarin
The Little Szechuan Place
in english
Shangri-la
this modest joint
serves taiwanese home cooking

pigs' ears, beef rolls, donuts
for dipping in soy milk

*

air thick
with lilac
the strong sun liquefying
the street

*

mosquito whine
dinner time

*

mourning dove at evening

and the ancients thought Venus

two stars equally bright
at morning and evening

doubling the source
of day's beauty

*

your plum lips
your slim hips
fingertips

*

and while I was not thinking
the lake rolled on

and while I was thinking
on a soft summer day sitting by the lake
I missed the lake

*

with my swizzle stick
and my scissor kick
I'm set for summer
drinks on the deck
and dives from the dock

the main halyard's new
nylon white and blue
the old mainsail's patched
no mice in the hatch

let's cast off from the dock
and break out the bock
set sail for Split Rock

*

reached for a raspberry
got a nettle

forgot the stove flame
burnt the old kettle

*

caffe latte—"caf
or decaf?" little choices
of an afternoon

stars arranging . . .

stars arranging themselves
according to old myths

blinking their fame
to the newest fans of the cosmos

o you are so fabulous
I could die of it!

what am I
if I lie

below the earth
below the sky

if burned to rise
to ash the sky

would the question be
not how but why

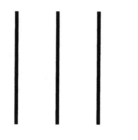

after guston II

with a trashcan lid in one hand
    and a broken stick in the other

a paper hat atop my head
    I will charge you rush you

lay you flat on the street
    a manhole cover your halo

Tenancy

The old Irish aunts are dead
  and thank god!
    —They were plagues
      on their nephew
  himself a plague
    on me his upstairs neighbor
  prey to his paranoiac riffs
    on nuns and shadowy city officials
      and his sister
    the absentee landlord.

Kinship's not all
  it's cracked up etcetera!
    If he forgets
      his dose he might lose it
    as he once unloosed his fists upon the admittedly
      querulous aunts
        the neighbors report.

But thankful we are
  for those spinsters
    he allegedly pummeled not least

for keeping one known malcontent
    home: they gardened and tended and now the dead

their roses and asters and bleeding hearts
    are blooming year after
        each crazy year.

MAYAKOVSKY at High Table

So many bottles of red wine drunk, nay plowed into

like Polish fields/girls pounded by Cossacks

my friend!!

—Is it not so?

Or did you mean to be a cenozoic creep

flicking your fins like that

in the late candlelight?

Blame it on the wine!

they brayed

tiny penises erect

below their pointed beards—

I swear I hadn't seen such a gathering

since Thomas Jefferson dined alone

with Sally Hemings!

Thus I sing my little song

(which you will not blame me for my friend)

in honor

of the fabulous wine cellar

only the elect may enter:

"One drop, one little drop . . ."

Terrible things are happening . . .

Terrible things are happening
                    in Russian novels!

    Just yesterday I heard
                    in the café

            of two peasants, long friends,

        one in sudden possession
                    of a watch
                            hanging
                                from a gold chain

        which so disturbed his compadre
                        he stole
            upon the other unsuspecting, prayed
                    to god

            and slit his throat, fleeing
                        with the watch—
                and that's not the worst of it!

Just yesterday my love and I too

            had not exactly a "fight"

    but a "reckoning"

         perhaps, or no—a

              "conversation" which opened the ocean

             of grief

    and now she is in another city

         perhaps crying

             and not because of Russian novels

My dearest Lavinia . . .

My dearest Lavinia I must confess
I do not wish to speak with you any more
about your impossible love, its excruciation,
her sloppy emotions and deft hesitation.
All this is true and has been excellently limned
and deserves, I am sure, further study.
Still you must admit the old light
in your eyes has turned somewhat feral
and thus it is no surprise your friends fear
you have birthed a wild obsession
that will torture more than you
all winter.

to a poet renowned for

a certain sensualism

and you
> with the world-historical orgasms
> you never fail to report
> in one of four languages
what have you to tell us
about pleasure

> which for you = the world
> and more, the endless figure
> of the world

say it wasn't your fingering soul
> made the world
nor your fabulous mind unfurling
> its ostentatiously various sails
> > on the world's several seas
nor the orgy of filaments spun
> from your profligate black deeps
> > linked the spheres suspended
> in space by their spinning musics

nothing to do with your plucking
      your fucking your gorgeous wallow
      luxurious sorrows aestheticized tragedies
      memories etcetera

you slid right along unknowing
      the deep granite face
      that resists all blandishings

Spatchcocked

A spatchcocked fowl is "split open and
grilled after being killed, plucked,
and dressed in a summary fashion."

—Oxford English Dictionary

I come to you today to speak not of cocks
per se or personal cocks impersonally borne by persons becocked
not at conception but later when cells are cracking so as to make
    cocks
abounding to the grace of cocky
sinners—viz. the slick celeb photog who's packed and stacked
    his cock
in his tight jeans just to the crotchseam's left, head cocked
to see if you notice. I notice. One hears these days that American
    cocks
are split, 50-50, but crack statisticians track 70% cocks
cut to 30% un- and rising. In careful countries cocks
go free unbothered by cleaver cook or other cocks
competing for chickies' company or the clear comforts of a large
    pen, good food, congenial cocks
they needn't peck to death. A fighting cock's
life's sad, it's hard, its legs steel-spurred yes everyone knows
    cocks
ain't too smart, cackling they are with only hens to cock

their crowns at. Today the gun's locked, loaded, cocked
and ready, yesterday my life had stood a loaded gun of cock-
amamie crap. Countryfolk calibrate the coming light by cock-
crow; some courtesans courted comtes and vicomtes to carry
    them through their economic cock-
ups. We know that Lorena Bobbitt bobbed it, a cruel blow: to lop
    a cock's
crazy exclaimed the cops who could lay their hands on a cock
from a number of red perspectives. Having surveyed millions
    of cocks
across the speculum's spectrum, I can say clearly, Alfred
    Hitchcock
took the prize—*¿por qué?* Wait till the third cock
croaks the sun up, I'll tell you. The blank ticktock, the screw
    and grind, the cock-
and-bull story that jerk jumped you with—a cripple cocks
his head, then he's dead; a spatchcocked cock
is killed plucked split and grilled. French cuisine perfected *coq*
au vin; Irish cooks cooked cocks
spatchcocked when sudden guests gathered at gates: cock-
sure standing there at the door they are, half-cocked
with their half-choked half-baked chicken bones some drunk'll
    cluck clear out of 'em.

Excursion Susan Sontag

Now Susan Sontag was famous
among certain people—you know
who I mean—urban informed culturally
literate East Coast people and some West
a few in Chicago in Europe and elsewhere although
Susan Sontag came from Arizona
which is remarkable
only if you hold certain prejudices
about Arizona which I do
having been there twice
and disliking it both times
not that this was Arizona's fault
it is majestic strange lunar orange desert
flat and then ravine-ridden but Phoenix
is heinous unless you have a certain
po-mo sensibility I associate with men
of a certain age and race and while
I share the supposed race I'm not a man although
there are men in Arizona but I forgot
to ask them what they thought
about the state or Susan Sontag
whose writings between 1964 and '67

are marvels of incisive thought and style
so much so that you have to wonder
what happened to America
what happened to Susan Sontag
who later published historical novels
in a realist mode when earlier she
championed the *nouveau roman*
oh where art thou where art thou Robbe-Grillet
and did her execution fail
her once-held prose ideals
oh is it our fate thus to lapse
if lapse it was and where is Sontag
to show us how to read Sontag
a professorial enthusiast
ringingly declared one Sunday Susan
"is always of the moment"
and thus we must conclude that in 1965
the new novel and criticism and sexy brains and France
were of the moment and now degraded realism
is of the moment as is "ethnic cleansing"
which Susan Sontag denounced indeed "put her life
on the line" (viz. enthusiast) producing Beckett
in Sarajevo she among the few
who spoke truly after 9/11 while torpor
overtook so many everyone waiting
for American Special Forces to "smoke"
Osama bin Laden "out of his hole"

on this matter Susan Sontag
held strong views e.g. about the president's
speech but she properly oriented us
to the club of men and one woman who advise him
since as she observed in an interview
on salon.com we are living in "a regency"
and we all know that regents are puppets
of their wily advisers cf. The Prince Regent
in England 1819 when aggrieved workers
gathered in Manchester and police agents
shot them tens hundreds dead maybe thousands
the papers covering up the massacre
whither media complicity is history now
and in England the people I met read several papers
expecting to compare and contrast each paper's
"take" on the news they didn't simply succumb
to the infantile American fantasy of media
"objectivity" the English and Irish
and Scots were like Burke unafraid
of prejudice they understood
you read through/with/against others'
prejudices and your own and thus Burke
against himself may be seen as an Enlightenment
theorist he supported the American Revolution
after all though he hysterically denounced
the French long before they guillotined anyone
o sweet Marie your fair chopped head

your luscious body the French pornographers
delighted in fucking tormenting reviling there
is a long affair between Enlightenment
philosophy and pornography as Cathleen Schine
explored in her spiky novel *Rameau's Niece*
as Sontag explored in a brilliant essay
of 1967 why are we so afraid
of porn there are many reasons the obvious
Freudian ones the "porn is rape" ones
the "protecting our children" ones the fear
of desire for the tabooed the "*jouissance*
of transgression" the world could blow up
any time but at the end
of the day it may all come down
to this our desire for knowledge
rips open the throat whole countries
have been seized with murder when threatened
with free inquiry not that those
who affiliate themselves self-righteously
with knowledge are not guilty of their own
simplifications because knowledge cuts
and opens wounds and distances
between lovers parents children citizens the world
feels different for example if you know
that somewhere people think god is dead
if the earth revolves around the sun
if you have stolen the gift of fire

if you know where your clitoris is and what
it can do and if you've seen Mapplethorpe's
whip stuck up his ass or his little devil's horns
perkily perched atop his mop of hair
why does he look so innocently rakish
is it because he's dead or that moment is or
is it my own perspective makes him so
not everything can be domesticated
or can it why did Proust avoid discussing
really discussing the mother now there is a crucial
evasion in an otherwise exhaustive
registration of the movements of consciousness
in society must old rockers and ACT UP veterans
and the Situationist International and Sontag all go
gentle into no that good that no that raging

Populating Heaven

If we belonged
to the dead, if we had our own
Egyptian culture of care—
the amulets of home entombed
for solace elsewhere—
would we then have found
a better way to cast beyond
the merely given earth?
        If you want to follow me
you'd better leave your plaid
suitcase and makeup kit
behind. I hope you won't
mind the narrow corridor;
the air in the chamber's
thinned out. In this dark
I think my life's an old hinge
creaking in silence.
        Open the door
and you'll see the creatures
I imagined while you were waiting:
the green-eyed dog upright
on his throne, the winged lion,

the woman whose third eye
brightens the room.
She's grinding lapis to paint
the veins of her breast.
Her nipples are coated with gold.
        It's true they rarely speak
but you're welcome
to ask their names.
Most days they lie
and dream among the harps.

They suffice
for themselves, neither
giving nor receiving.

See how they wither
in the momentary glance,
turn to dust on the
steps we climbed
to get here.

There is a place . . .

There is a place in the world
for cracked things: the wedding
glass, the Zuni jar

you dropped, my poor idea
of god. Hear
how my voice breaks

in the highest register?

At the end, a door

I walked through

and on the other side
I thought I'd look back

through the door
"that was another life"

here I am
on this side standing looking

same life

§

What for
this failure

the outline
of the beloved

body haunting sleep
fleshing itself out of nothing

what for this failure love

§

Certain voices linger
in the mind as in the ear

a pitch rings
the soul forked

in regular intervals
"a life of affections and apprehensions"

this was beatitude

§

"To be released from desperation
about love" and other wishes.

Only the disenchanted
are free. So you said to me.

Have I elected this liberty

are we so simply thrust

into the blank

§

"But you are young"
and other ruses.

Who's to say
what's new, what's worth

losing. I excuse
almost nothing.

I wrote my soul
in a red book, lost it

in a strange city.
I will never speak again

of keeping

§

And other outworn terms
such as sacred

I admit I swoon
I told no one

but I could not deny
I would rather lie

abased than lie
alone

so I once said
false extravagance

§

the low black cloud
that hangs below

your crystal mind
has tried my faith

the lucid word false
the careful tongue taut

longing aborted

§

who can afford to sustain
the call note

to call out again
your name

error no error
wandering we went

hand in hand
slow steps

§

how would I call to you
if I could call to you

your brittle name would break
if I should get it wrong

I still wear the ring
I should forgo

my breast hollow
breath shallow

nipples pierced with pins
you'll never touch

§

on whom
do your long fingers rest

on whose breast
and whose face
do your eyes reflect

in the dark

I suspect

your back curves
to a new body

§

and I who had abandoned
worship

secular transposition
the body for the holy

all the old reverence
reaching for its object

yes lord I was grateful

and you the occasion
unwitting

§

a new kind of waiting
breathless alert

hope punched my heart

lying face / down . . .

lying face
down in the
grass the blades'
imprint
my cheek
my thigh
each surface
recording
what touches
it best
so close

grass my skin
you my heart

syntax

and if
I were to say

I love you and
I do love you

and I say it
now and again

and again
would you say

parataxis
would you see

the world revolves
anew

its axis
you

song

o light is love
its matchless beauty shining
and light my heart her voice
my heart inclining

o sweet is love
her flash my body burning
and sweet her tongue my tongue
her body learning

early music at the coffee shop

a harpsichord, a lute & then
a brace
of trumpets flying

on the wings of your melisma

harmony
a late
development

and rhythms
not the waves of the sea

but a human pulse
toward form

I wanted to crawl inside . . .

I wanted to crawl inside a middle voice
of a Tallis motet and sleep

the centuries away but the promise
of a cadence lured me awake

in the woods the air aflutter
with alien birds seeking a branching grace.

there was a form for beseeching
and a form for praising

never too far from the anchor
never too far from the shore

and now a passing note
blows the body into another world

mist lowering the scrim . . .

mist lowering the scrim
on the day

all the moored boats in the cove
seeming to drift

awaiting
their mortal passengers

symphony / in the air . . .

symphony
in the air

contending
with the wind

and winning—
its bandwidth

broad—beethoven
ever beating

the clements

notational / sufficiency . . .

notational
sufficiency: a wager

made some days
attention

seems wholly
enough

despite the danger
of a simplified

syntax, a mere
gleaning

from the surround—

so thought
hovered,

unstreaming,
punctual, rough

cumuli gathering low . . .

cumuli gathering low
& graywashed below
the faint blue tiepolo
openings. a possible frost
predicted. definite
autumn. even the days
the sun don't come out
the sun came somewhere
up. a *soft somer*
season nearly
over. another so
long song. another
hummingbird probing
the bleeding heart's heart.

was he right . . .

was he right the poet
who said *memory*—

recovery of the lost—
this is what poetry—

right now the crickets
are pulsing above

a steady stream
of traffic just beyond the hedge

and I am remembering
nothing

same view . . .

same view
same long lush lawn

same three tall maples and their lower kin
same windwashed lake

and beyond, the immemorial mountain

the sleeping granite man
still keeps his giant sleep

but I have come back
and I am not she

Core Samples

When I met you I was eighteen
bitter as the bolted lettuce
neglected in the garden.
Your laugh had a hiss.

You lay in the bathtub
choosing between me and her,
both of us singers.
For some reason she would not sleep with you.

That was long ago.
You have a young daughter,
another wife.
I am sure you never tell her

how it was with us.
You were always discreet.
Now I sit by roses
not missing you and your long silences.

§

Those were the years I fell in love
with every woman I knew.
All my close friends touched my tongue
at least once, then returned to their sensible husbands.

Sometimes we arrange to meet
and after some wine they remember
and blush and wonder
and ask if I too wonder.

It seemed one could be anyone
those liquid nights.
I now walk by a river with my lover
and they go to their several homes
carefully shutting the doors.

§

It was under the spell of Yeats I fell
in love with you, though it may have gone back
to Chaucer. One night I had a dream
I was a heroine in Spenser

and woke up burnt, branded
by your imagined touch.
There came a day in spring
when stung by your faithless lover

you were more than ready for another.
That day we read no further.

You wanted to be seduced.
At that time I could not play master.
Your breathing got faster
as you leaned, desperate, into your desired disaster.

§

You I never fell in love with.
I confess it was an experiment
and perhaps unfair. In my defense
let it be said I experimented more

on me than you, who were already beholden
to your "erotics of surprise."
I did not wish to be surprised.
With you I saw how far I could go

away from myself. On the open ocean
the sun beats hard and true
and your thirst is never relieved
except by what you bring with you.

You gave me to know this
and gave me an illness

you didn't even know
you had. They tell me
you're never wholly cured.

§

I never made you breakfast.
Thank you for the coffee and the toast,
the encouragement to get the piano
—but let's forget the rest.

It was never about lust
you sd, thrilled to be so honest
and casual by the lake.
I thought you were a fake.

I was sick of your music
and sick of the sex
that was rarely more than anemic,
a studied thrust & suck.

Still it amazes me
after that talk
and the lake turning black
you thought I'd come back.

§

Sad in bed you read Horace
the ode in which an aging lover pleads
not to be inflamed again
by a perishable love

and a tear escapes his eye
and a tear escaped your eye.
I was wild for you and heedless
I am glad love to say this

I was afflicted and afflicted you.
Be careful what you wish for
you warned. I was not careful
nor in the end thank god were you.

The charms I recited
the songs I sang
were lit by a light
almost wholly impersonal.

Yet what are we but vehicles
of waves we never directly perceive
except those days the light bending
around our bodies becomes our body
—the lovers ablaze on the pyre

do I still turn to them . . .

do I still turn to them the dead
who speak in type the way the sun
bursts between the legs those days
a tongue moves so—what diction
love what thirst what level bed to lay
myself upon when dawn is where
we're going with the sun

in the end a windblown woman . . .

in the end a windblown woman am I
and all the others too thinned out

: of the bones: whitened forms writing
against the garish hillside—

whence the trumpeters? and the lone high flute?
only some days did we realize

the bless of the body the babies
the athletes the lovers shining

their unredeemable flesh

Envoi

Go litel myn book
and blow her head off

make her retch and weep
        and ache in the gut

make her regret everything about her life
        that doesn't include me

NOTES

"Catches for Robert Duncan": see Duncan's *The Years as Catches: Early Poems, 1939–1946* (Berkeley: Oyez, 1966).

"From Mz N: the serial": John Pinkerton (1758–1826), a literary antiquarian, forger, numismatist, and crank.

"Poem": Julian of Norwich, fourteenth-century English mystic. She is the author of *Revelations of Divine Love.*

"At the end, a door": "a life of affections and apprehensions" and the surrounding lines are a paraphrase and transposition of a passage in William of Auvergne's *The Immortality of the Soul* [*De immortalitate animae*], trans. Roland J. Teske, S.J. (Milwaukee: Marquette University Press, 1991), p. 55: "Thus it is in the life of beatitude, because, when the mind is wholly caught up in God and removed from all other things, it will draw its whole life from him alone and will pour it all back and return it to him, because life consists wholly in apprehensions and affections."

ACKNOWLEDGMENTS

I am grateful to the editors of the following journals, in which some of these poems first appeared, sometimes in slightly different form: *American Letters & Commentary, The Canary, Circumference: Poetry in Translation, Harvard Review, Jacket, The New Yorker,* and *Slate.* Several poems in this book appeared in the chapbook *This Carrying Life* (Boston: Arrowsmith Press, 2005) and in *This Carrying Life II* (Boston: Pressed Wafer and Arrowsmith, 2006), an expanded second edition of the chapbook, which included poems previously published in a Pressed Wafer broadside of April 2005.

I would like to thank the Corporation of Yaddo and Hedgebrook for their generosity and support: parts of this book were written during the residencies they sponsored.

For "the knowing, / the being and being here," best thanks to Jonathan Galassi; and my gratitude as well to August Kleinzahler; to Erica Mena and Devin Johnston; and to Alane Rollings and Julia Targ, steadfast always.

This book is dedicated with admiration to William Corbett and to Askold Melnyczuk. And, first and last, *à elle.*